LP Project Box

ST. BENEDICT'S JUNIOR SCHOOL
EALING, W.5.

Accession No.
Classification

HOW THEY LIVED

A ROMAN GLADIATOR

ANNE STEEL

*Illustrated by
Peter Chesterton*

HOW THEY LIVED

An American Pioneer Family
An Australian Pioneer
An Aztec Warrior
A Celtic Family
A Child in Victorian London
A Colonial American Merchant
A Crusading Knight
An Edwardian Household
A Family in the Fifties
A Family in the Thirties
A Family in World War I
A Family in World War II
An Ice Age Hunter
An Inca Farmer
A Medieval Monk
A Medieval Serf
A Norman Baron

A Plains Indian Warrior
A Plantation Slave
A Roman Centurion
A Roman Gladiator
A Sailor with Captain Cook
A Samurai Warrior
A Saxon Farmer
A Schoolchild in World War II
A Slave in Ancient Greece
A Soldier in Wellington's Army
A Soldier in World War I
A Suffragette
A Teenager in the Sixties
A Tudor Merchant
A Victorian Factory Worker
A Viking Sailor

Editor: Amanda Earl

First published in 1988 by
Wayland (Publishers) Limited
61 Western Road, Hove
East Sussex BN3 1JD, England

© Copyright 1988 Wayland (Publishers) Ltd

All the words that appear in **bold** in the text are explained in the glossary on page 31.

British Library Cataloguing in Publication Data

Steel, Anne
A Roman gladiator. – (How they lived).
1. Gladiators – Juvenile literature
2. Rome – Social life and customs – Juvenile literature
I. Title II. Chesterton, Peter III. Series
394'.8'0937   GV35

ISBN 1 85210 314 0

Phototypeset by Kalligraphics Ltd, Redhill, England
Printed and bound in Belgium by Casterman S.A.

CONTENTS

BRAVE FIGHTERS 4

WHO WERE THE GLADIATORS? 6

TYPES OF GLADIATORS 8

PREPARING FOR THE ARENA 10

THE COLOSSEUM 12

THE GAMES 14

MORTAL COMBAT 16

REWARDS FOR VICTORY 18

ENTERTAINMENT 20

LIVING IN THE CITY 22

FOOD AND DRINK 24

CLOTHES AND APPEARANCE 26

RELIGION 28

THE END OF THE GLADIATORS 30

GLOSSARY 31

MORE BOOKS TO READ 31

INDEX 32

BRAVE FIGHTERS

A fanfare of horns rang out over the packed **amphitheatre**. Murmurs of excitement passed through the huge crowd as two gladiators stepped from the shadows into the blinding sun of the arena. One was tall and powerful, the other short and lightly built. The bigger man carried a heavy sword and a massive shield; the other was armed with a net, a **trident** and a razor-sharp dagger. They stood face to face, glaring at each other as their weapons were checked for sharpness. Then the signal was given for the fight to begin.

Below *A Roman statue of Titus Flavius, Emperor of Rome from AD 78–81. He encouraged gladiator contests.*

The crowd shouted with excitement as the two men circled warily around each other, waiting for an opening. A lunging sword thrust was easily avoided by the smaller man, who jabbed at his opponent with the trident, grazing his bare hand. The crowd roared at the first sight of blood. For several minutes the contest continued, then the net whirled through the air, leaving its victim struggling beneath it like a helpless insect. The trident rose and fell, and the frenzied crowd screamed their approval at the first kill of the afternoon.

The year was AD 80 and Titus was Emperor of the **Roman Empire** at the time. The gladiator fight was part of the games celebrating the opening of the **Colosseum** in Rome. The Romans loved these bloodthirsty spectacles and in this book you can read about the games and the men who fought in them – the gladiators.

Opposite *Gladiators of different skills fought each other. Here, a Samnite and a Retiarius entertain a packed arena.*

WHO WERE THE GLADIATORS?

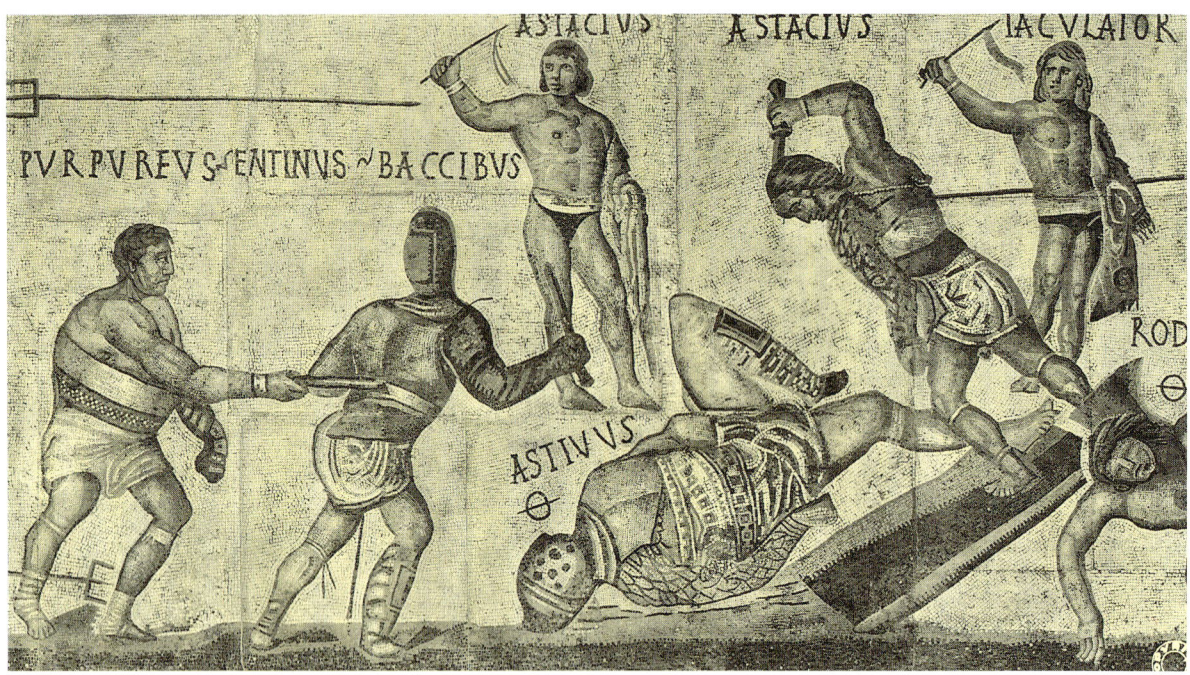

Gladiators were trained fighters who entertained people in special arenas as part of the Roman games. Their lives were usually short – duels were fought to the death unless the crowds took pity on a beaten man. Few gladiators lived to fight in more than two or three contests.

Most of the men were slaves, criminals or prisoners of war, who had little or no hope of wealth or freedom. They chose the life of the training schools and risked death in the arena in return for the chance of riches, freedom and fame.

A beautiful Roman mosaic from the fourth century AD, showing several groups of gladiators in combat. It can be seen today in the Galleria Borghese, outside Rome.

Some of the gladiators were free men who enjoyed the thrill of fighting in front of thousands of people. Young men from wealthy families sometimes ran away to join the training schools, but most of the men did not become gladiators by choice.

Gladiators were placed under the control of gladiator trainers. They swore an **oath** of **obedience**: 'I undertake to be burned by fire, to be chained, to be beaten and to die by the sword.'

A small ancient terracotta statue of two fighting gladiators from the first century AD.

Serious training took up most of the gladiators' time.

Types of Gladiators

Not all gladiators had the same weapons or armour. There were different classes of fighter, depending on the size, strength and skill of each man.

Large, strong men were trained to become Murmillo or Samnite gladiators. Such men used short, thick swords, huge, rectangular shields and leg and arm-guards. The Murmillones often wore helmets crowned with a fish shape. The Samnites' helmets had a crest and a tuft of feathers on the top. Such helmets were as much for decoration as protection, as the **visors** sometimes made it difficult for the gladiators to see clearly.

The Retiarii and the Thracian gladiators were lightly-armed, and used speed and **agility** to defeat stronger men. The Retiarii (like the smaller gladiator on page 4) fought

This Roman stone relief shows three Samnite gladiators.

Above *The decoration on this Samnite's helmet, depicts a scene from a Roman war.*
Above right *This helmet was probably worn by a Murmillo gladiator. The visor often made it difficult to see.*

A highly decorated dagger and sheath of the type used by lightly armed Retiarii gladiators.

with a net, trident and dagger. The Thracians were armed with a small, round shield and a razor-sharp curved sword.

Other classes of gladiator included the Andabtae, who fought in armour on horseback, and the Essedarii, who fought from war chariots. To make the contests more exciting, gladiators of different kinds were set against each other. The Retiarii fought against the Murmillones and Thracians battled with Samnites.

The games might last for many days, during which time hundreds of men would meet their deaths in the arena. In AD 108, as many as 4,971 pairs of gladiators fought during 117 days of games.

PREPARING FOR THE ARENA

The gladiators lived in three special training schools in Rome. The largest was called the **Ludus Magnus**. It was very close to the Colosseum, where most of the games took place. Many of the gladiators had been used to hard lives as slaves, prisoners or criminals, and they welcomed the life of the training schools. They were kept comfortable, well fed and clothed and were able to leave the training schools in the afternoon to socialize. If they were successful in winning a fight in the arena, they were rewarded with riches.

This Roman mosaic, found at Bignor Roman Villa in Sussex, shows two gladiators training. A Retiarius gladiator is on the right.

The names of the different types of gladiators were derived from enemies of the Roman Empire. These beautiful miniature statues of the period show the heavily armed Samnites.

Above *This small stone statue, found at Pompeii, is thought to depict a gladiator (with the helmet) and his trainer.*

The schools were well equipped. There were **masseurs** and doctors to help keep the men fit. The trainers often were former gladiators who had survived the arena to pass on their knowledge. They were often scarred or maimed in some way.

The gladiators were first shown the main fighting skills, and then taught the art of a particular class of fighter. They were also taught to fight from boats, as the arena could be flooded for naval battles! New recruits were always joining the schools to replace dead men.

Before the games, a huge feast was held for the gladiators. For many of them it was their last meal. Some ate and drank freely, some ate more carefully, thinking of the fighting to follow the next day. A few were too scared to eat or drink at all.

THE COLOSSEUM

The Colosseum was a huge stone-built oval amphitheatre where the games took place in Rome. It took ten years to build, and was opened in AD 80 by the Emperor Titus with games that lasted for 100 days.

The Colosseum was so strongly built that most of it still stands today. It had four storeys, reaching up to a height of 50 m. There were 80 entrances and seats for around 45,000 people, with room for 5,000 standing.

The inside of the arena was 86 m long and 54 m wide. The seats began 4 m above the arena to protect the crowd from the fighters and wild animals. The first twenty rows were for the rich and important; the rest of the crowd filled the seats behind. The Emperor and his family had their own special viewing box.

The building was carefully designed, with many passageways and staircases to and from the seats. On hot days, a canvas roof was pulled out around the rim of the building to shield the arena, and the people, from the sun.

Beneath the Colosseum there were animal **enclosures** and lifts to bring them to the arena when needed.

A cut-away view of the Colosseum and its surrounding area.

THE GAMES

The Roman custom of holding games was very old. Originally they were held in memory of someone who had died, or in honour of the gods. By the end of the first century AD, however, the religious side was less important and the games were mainly for entertainment. Also, the Emperor and other powerful men

At the games, gladiators also fought wild animals such as leopards.

sometimes used the games to win support and gain popularity. Gradually the number of games held each year grew, and they lasted longer.

The games were full of cruelty and bloodshed, yet the crowds came in their thousands. The gladiatorial fights were the most popular, though there were plenty of other events to hold the interest of the crowds.

Trained animals performed circus tricks. For example, cheetahs might pull chariots. Many different animals were made to fight one another. There were duels between bears and buffalo, elephants and rhinos, lions and bears and other animals from all over the Roman Empire. These included wild **boar**, bulls, leopards, ostriches and apes.

This scene shows animals being caught for the games.

Sometimes animals were let into the arena and shot at by archers safe in iron cages. Armed men also hunted them with hungry dogs. During one day, hundreds of animals might be cruelly slaughtered.

Animals were also used to kill unarmed men and women in the arena. Many of these people were Christians, who were **persecuted** by the Romans.

Entry to the games was probably by a theatre token like this. The letters are thought to indicate the person's seat number.

MORTAL COMBAT

Before the gladiator contests began, the fighters paraded into the arena with **valets** carrying their weapons. They saluted the President of the Games, often the Emperor, with the words: 'Hail, Emperor, those who are about to die salute you.'

Sometimes there were mock battles with wooden or **muffled** weapons before the real fights. These did not last long, for the crowd grew impatient and called for action. Then, the real weapons were checked for sharpness, and a fanfare was played as the first men entered the arena. Often only one duel was fought at a time. Sometimes many went on together.

Below *A heavy iron shield used by some of the gladiators for protection.*

Above *A gladiator's short-sword, or dagger, made from iron, bone and ivory.*

The crowd placed bets on their favourites and screamed for blood. Each duel ended when a gladiator was killed or when one of them gave up the fight. The loser might lie on his back and beg for mercy. Then the crowd would give the thumbs up or thumbs down sign. The President had to decide whether the beaten man lived or died, but he rarely went against the will of the people. Thumbs up and the man left the arena alive; thumbs down and he was finished off with one swift stroke of the sword.

The dead gladiators were dragged from the ring with ropes and metal hooks. The bodies were thrown into carts and dumped in mass graves.

The gladiators parade into the arena and are announced to the crowd.

REWARDS FOR VICTORY

Each victorious gladiator received prizes from the President of the Games, or a politician. They were given gold and silver bowls, or trays filled with gold coins and other gifts.

A former slave, prisoner of war or criminal might suddenly find himself rich, and a hero with the crowds. Sadly, he rarely lived long enough to enjoy his new wealth and popularity. He had to fight again, and was often killed in his very next duel.

An umpire of the fights holds a 'Rudis' in his hand. If a gladiator won five fights he was awarded this symbol and gained his freedom.

If a gladiator won five fights in a row, he won the wooden symbol or 'Rudis' and became a free man. But many refused to accept the sword, and continued to take their chances in the arena. The thrill of winning and the thought of more riches made them want to fight again. One man, named Flamma, was presented with the Rudis four times, but he chose to remain a gladiator until he was killed in his twenty-second fight.

Some men did choose freedom, and the chance to enjoy their earnings. They often became trainers, passing on their skills to new generations of fighters.

A coin from the Emperor Titus period. Gladiators were rewarded with such coins.

The Emperor awards a victorious gladiator a gold bowl. He would also receive a palm leaf as a symbol of his success.

ENTERTAINMENT

The Romans loved watching chariot races, which were almost as dangerous as the gladiator contests.

The races were held in the **Circus Maximus**, on a rectangular track which had semi-circular turns at each end. The Circus could seat about 250,000 people, or about a quarter of the population of Rome. The seats were free, so the crowds began to arrive before dawn to get the best places.

Chariot races were extremely popular, as this painting from the second century AD shows.

About twelve races were held each day between the different teams of chariots. The crowd, including many gladiators, placed bets on their favourites and waved scarves to show which team they supported – red, blue, white or green.

The two-wheeled, wood and leather chariots were usually pulled by two or four horses. The charioteers rode standing up, with the reins wound round their bodies. The chariots were allowed to bump each other and there were many accidents. Charioteers were often badly injured and many were killed.

There were other, less violent, entertainments too. Most Romans went to the public baths each day, men in the afternoon, and women in the morning. They went there to get clean, relax, meet with friends and get fit. There were sports areas for athletics, wrestling and ball games. After such exercise, people relaxed in the baths, which ranged from cold to very hot. There were also shops, reading rooms and libraries, gardens, art galleries and museums. The charge was so small that most people could afford to go. The gladiators enjoyed this relaxation too.

Above *The Roman Baths at Bath, England. Gladiators would have visited public baths similar to this each day.*

Above *An ancient Roman gaming table. Gladiators would probably relax and play dice games some afternoons.*

Living in the City

In the centre of Rome was a large open space called the **Forum**, the main meeting place in the city. Around the Forum were magnificent buildings, statues, parks, baths, shops, warehouses and markets.

By the end of the first century AD, the population of Rome had reached one million. The city was too small for so many people, and it became cramped and noisy. Away from the centre, the streets were narrow and dirty, and buildings were taller to save space.

The tall buildings were called **insulae**. They were up to five storeys high. Almost everyone lived in these flats. They were not well built and often fell down!

In the narrow lanes people crowded to the shops which opened on to the street. Each shop sold only one kind of goods. Barbers sat their customers in the street, beggars called out, **hawkers** cried out their wares and small crowds gathered round street entertainers. Friends met in the taverns to enjoy a drink and hot, cheap food.

The city was not lit at night and most people stayed in their homes. Rich people went out with slaves to protect them and light the way. But the city was not quiet at night, for wheeled vehicles moved about. Rome was too small to cope with traffic and people at the same time, so vehicles were forbidden in the daytime. Sleeping at night could be difficult in Rome!

This is the Arch of Titus in Rome. Built in the first century AD, it was once the gateway from the Forum to the Colosseum.

Opposite *A view through the insulae in Rome. The backstreets of the city were noisy, crowded and dirty.*

FOOD AND DRINK

The first meal of the day for the gladiators was eaten around dawn. It was a simple meal of bread and cheese. The next meal was at the end of the morning, after the main training period. Bread, cheese, meat and fruit were eaten with a little wine, which was often diluted with water.

The main meal was eaten around four o'clock in the afternoon, perhaps

Below *The remains of a triclinium in Pompeii. A triclinium was a type of Roman dining room which had couches around a table for eating. Gladiators would have had some meals in such a room.*

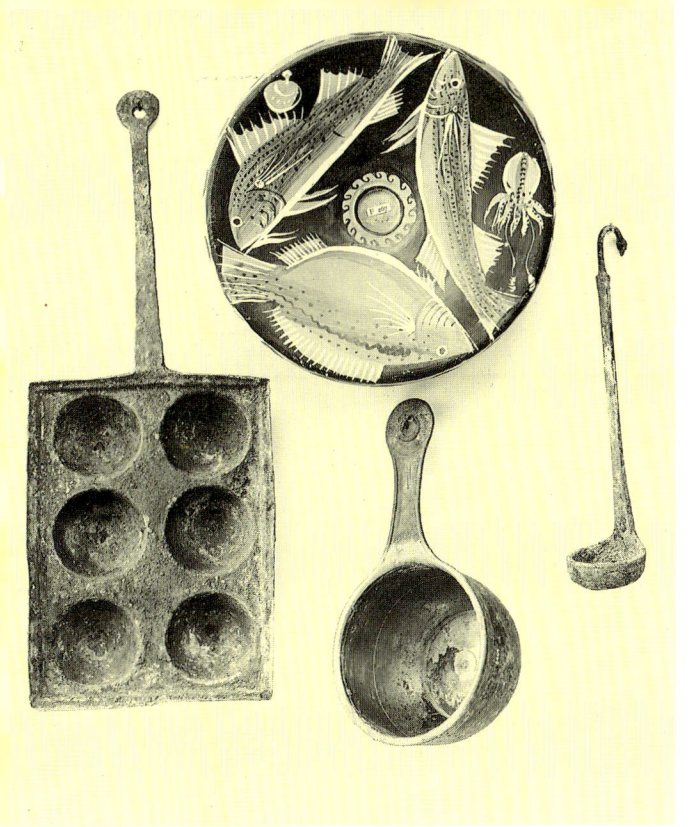

Above *Some Roman kitchen artefacts, including a plate, some ladles and an early baking tray.*

Above *A typical gladiators' banquet. Such meals were held before each contest.*

after a trip to the baths. This was the biggest meal, and would include fish, meat, vegetables, fruit and wine. The Romans ate most of the meats we eat today, as well as others such as **crane**, wild boar and wild goat.

Before each gladiator contest, men went to a large banquet where there were at least three courses. The starters might be boiled tree fungi, sea urchins with spices and honey, or sows' udders stuffed with nuts and pine kernels. Wine was drunk all through the banquet. The Romans ate with their fingers, using a knife and spoon to help them. They had to wash their hands between courses.

Gladiators would eat from pottery bowls like the ones below.

25

CLOTHES AND APPEARANCE

When they travelled to the Colosseum the gladiators dressed colourfully in purple cloaks embroidered with gold. Some of them wore highly polished armour underneath. The cloaks were worn for the parade and were taken off when the fights began.

Right *Gladiator leg-guards or greaves.*

Below *A stone relief showing the type of everyday clothes worn in Roman times.*

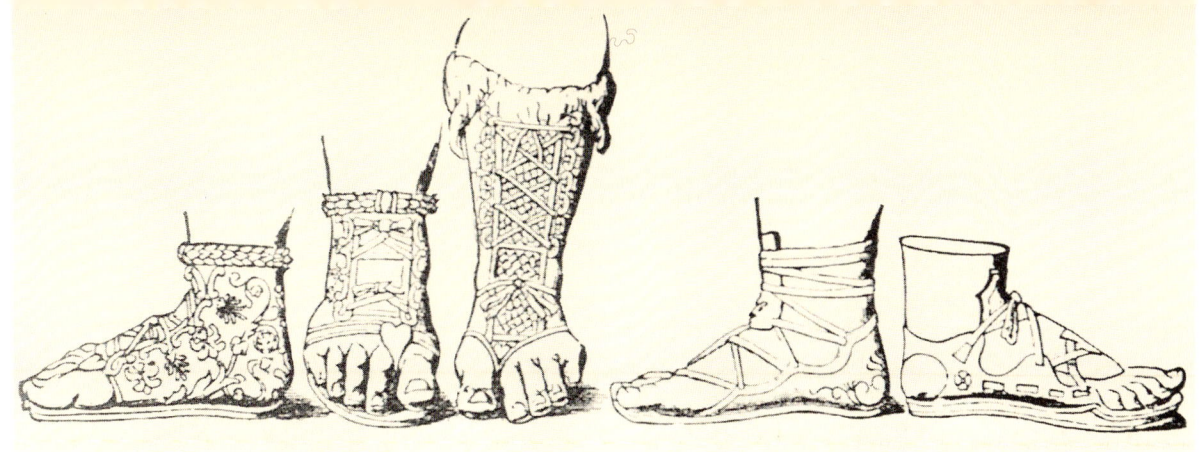

Above *Examples of shoes (calcaei) and sandals (sandalia) worn by the Romans and gladiators. The shoes on the left would have been for special occasions.*

During an ordinary day the men wore two simple garments. The first was a linen loincloth tied round the waist. A tunic was worn over this. The tunic was a simple garment, of linen or wool, which reached to above the knees. It was made by sewing two lengths of cloth together. It slipped over the head and was fastened round the waist with a belt. Tunics had short sleeves, so in cold weather more than one would be worn. The loin cloth and tunic were also worn at night.

Almost all men had short hair at this time, and only a small number grew beards. Rome was full of busy barber shops.

Once a gladiator had gained his freedom, he could wear a toga, the traditional Roman robe. This was a long, white cloth draped round the body in a very complicated way. Because it was so difficult to put on, many people wore togas only on special occasions.

Gladiators might also have worn good-luck charms. This pottery love-token was probably worn around the neck on a cord (note the small hole to the right). The inscription is 'Verecunda Ludia Lucius Gladiator'. *Verecunda is a Roman girl's name, and it is assumed she gave the token to Lucius, a gladiator, as a sign of her affection.*

RELIGION

There were many Roman gods and goddesses. The most important had temples built in their honour, where priests carried out sacrifices and ceremonies. Jupiter was the ruler of the gods, Mars the god of war, Juno the wife of Jupiter and the protector of women and Fortuna the goddess of good luck.

There were also household gods. People believed that they protected families from illness and bad luck. Most homes had a shrine in the hall where the family prayed each day.

By the end of the first century AD, few educated Romans still believed in the old gods. Many public festivals

A statue of the Roman god, Mars.

had begun in honour of the gods, but the religious part gradually became less important.

As the Roman Empire spread, people became interested in religions from other countries. Some became followers of the Persian god Mithras and the Egyptian goddess Isis.

A household shrine found at Pompeii.

Above *A stone relief showing a sacrifice in honour of a Roman god.*

Another cult was Emperor worship, which grew from the time of Julius Caesar. After his death in 44 BC he was called a god. Some Emperors after this time wished to be worshipped as gods in their lifetime as well as after death.

By the first century AD the number of Christians was growing, but they were **persecuted** for following the teachings of Christ and had to worship in secret. If they refused to worship the Roman state gods they were put to death.

A Roman statue of the Egyptian goddess, Isis. Many Romans began to worship foreign gods and goddesses.

The End of the Gladiators

Gladiatorial contests continued to be one of the most popular forms of entertainment for most of the period of the Roman Empire. Some of the Emperors, including Augustus and Domitian, tried to encourage people to watch Greek-style games, with athletic contests instead of the cruel Roman games, but the desire for bloodshed was too powerful. Most of the people showed little interest in efforts to interest them in less cruel entertainments. Other Emperors, including Hadrian and Marcus Aurelius, introduced mock combats in which no one was actually killed, but these did not satisfy a mob who had become used to real slaughter.

It was not until Christianity became the official religion of the Roman Empire that the games began to disappear. In AD 326 the Christian Emperor Constantine made it illegal for criminals to be punished by being sent into the arena, and by the end of the fourth century the games had disappeared altogether.

A piece of glass depicting a gladiator. Today, the gladiators way of life seems barbaric, but small relics such as this serve as a reminder of that period in Roman history.

GLOSSARY

Agility Nimble, quickness of movement.
Amphitheatre An oval or circular building with rows of seats rising above each other round a central open space.
Boar A male pig.
Circus Maximus A circular building in Rome with a track, where chariot races were held.
Colosseum A four-storey, oval building in Rome where games were held.
Crane Large wading bird with a long neck, legs and bill.
Enclosures Walled-in, secure areas.
Forum A large open space in Rome where people used to meet; originally a market place.
Hawkers People who sell goods in the street.
Insulae Tall, narrow buildings, where most poor Romans lived.

Ludus Magnus The largest of the gladiator training schools.
Masseurs People trained to give massages.
Oath A sworn promise.
Obedience To obey or carry out another's command or order.
Persecuted Subjected to unfair and unjust treatment due to religious beliefs.
Roman Empire The territories ruled by ancient Rome. Established by Augustus in 27 BC, the Empire grew to eventually include West and Southern Europe, Africa north of the Sahara and South-West Asia.
Trident A three-pronged spear.
Valet A manservant.
Visor The movable part of a helmet, covering the face.

MORE BOOKS TO READ

Jane Chisholm, *Living in Roman Times*, (Usborne, 1982)
Henry Pluckrose, *Romans*, (Hamish Hamilton, 1981)
R.J. Unstead, *A Roman Town*, (Hutchinson, 1977)
Barry and Anne Steel, *The Romans*, (Wayland, 1985)

F.R. Cowell, *Everyday Life in Ancient Rome*, (Batsford, 1961)
Joan Forman, *The Romans*, (Macdonald, 1975)
Clarence Greig, *Great Civilizations: Rome*, (Ladybird, 1974)
G.I.F. Tingay and J. Badcock, *These Were the Romans*, (Hulton, 1972)

INDEX

Amphitheatre 4, 12, 31
Animals 15
Arena, the 4, 10, 13

Caesar, Julius 29
Chariot races 9, 15, 20, 21
Christian persecution 15, 31
Christian religion 29, 30
Circus events 15
Circus Maximus 20, 31
Clothes 26–27
Colosseum, the 4, 10, 12–13, 26, 31
Constantine, Emperor 30

Duels 6, 16, 18

Entertainment and socializing 11, 21

Feasts and banquets 11, 24, 25
Fighting skills 11
Flamma, the gladiator 18
Food and drink 24–25
Forum, the 22, 31
Freedom 18, 27
Free men 7, 18

Games, the 4, 6, 9, 10, 12, 14–15
Gladiatorial fights 4, 9, 15, 16, 20, 24, 30
Gladiators,
  background of 6, 10
  end of the 30
  life expectancy of 6
  new recruits of 11
Gladiators, types of
  Andabtae 9
  Essedarii 9
  Murmillo 8
  Retiarii 8
  Samnite 8
  Thracian 8, 9
Gods and goddesses 15, 28–29

Insulae, the 22, 31

Living conditions 11, 22
Love-tokens and charms 27
Ludus Magnus 10, 31

Mock battles 16, 30

Naval battles 11

Oath of obedience 7, 31

Pastimes 21
Prisoners of war 6, 10, 18
Public baths 21, 24

Religion 15, 28–29
Rewards and prizes 11, 18–19
Roman Emperors 30
Roman Empire 4, 28, 30, 31
Rome 4, 12, 23
  population of 20, 22
'Rudis', the 18

Slaves 6, 10, 18, 22
Sports and athletics 21

Trainers, gladiator 11, 18
Training schools 6, 10, 11, 18
Titus, Emperor 4, 12, 13, 15

Valets 16

Weapons and armour 4, 8–9, 16, 26

Picture acknowledgements
The pictures in this book were supplied by the following: BBC Hulton Picture Library 25 (left); BPCC/Aldus Archive 8, 15; Bridgeman Art Library 24, 26 (below), 30; Leicestershire Museums, Art Galleries and Records Service (Jewry Wall Museum) 27 (below); The Mansell Collection 6, 9 (left), 14, 26 (above); Ronald Sheridan's Photo Library 4, 7, 9 (right), 10, 16 (right), 18 (both), 21 (right), 28 (both), 29 (below); Sonia Halliday Photographs 11 (left), 21 (left), 22, 29 (above); The Trustees of the British Museum 9 (below), 11 (right), 16 (left) 25 (below). The remaining pictures are from the Wayland Picture Library.